Cricket Widows

A Note About the Author

Noel Ford, creator of *Golf Widows,* learnt about cricket from his father who was a uniquely committed cricketer. While he batted and bowled his wife buttered and sliced – leaving the young Noel a cricket orphan.

Noel Ford now lives with his wife – a cartooning widow – and daughter in Leicestershire.

Cricket
Widows

PITCH BATTLES
BETWEEN THE SEXES

Foreword by Brian Johnston

NOEL FORD

ANGUS
& ROBERTSON
PUBLISHERS

ANGUS & ROBERTSON PUBLISHERS

16 Golden Square, London W1R 4BN,
United Kingdom, and
Unit 4, Eden Park, 31 Waterloo Road,
North Ryde, NSW, Australia 2113.

First published in the United Kingdom by
Angus & Robertson (UK) in 1989
First published in Australia by
Angus & Robertson Publishers in 1989

Copyright © Noel Ford, 1989

ISBN 0 207 16227 1

Typeset in UK by New Faces, Bedford

Printed in the United Kingdom

Contents

Foreword by
Brian Johnston

I ought to be an expert on cricket widows. I married one. (Though she's been de-cricket-widowed for the last twenty years since I gave up playing.)

When I first met my wife two things especially attracted me to her: she could throw a cricket ball like a man, and her great grandfather was a founder member of the Yorkshire County Cricket Club. Even so, she was a bit suspicious when she realised that our honeymoon had been timed to end on the very day of the start of the cricket season. But in the end – and like all good wives should (or so we cricketers think), she accompanied me to all my matches, for a good gossip with her fellow cricket widows, as well as to watch the match. As our family grew over the years, she used to bring them too to watch Daddy keeping wicket.

These matches were mostly on Sundays, as every Saturday I had tc go off somewhere to commentate on a county game or Test Match. Then after ten years I started to go on tours overseas, which did mean that she was left alone for long periods in the winter. But there were compensations. She used to join me for part of the tours, leaving the children behind in the charge of an aunt or her ex-headmistress. As a result she has been several times to

Australia, the West Indies, South Africa and New Zealand, and this does help to ease my conscience.

Some husbands, of course, carry their enthusiasm for the game too far; as in the famous story of the newly married young cricketer who, when shown up to the honeymoon suite on his wedding night gazed adoringly at his young bride and said, 'Shall we go straight to bed or do you think we could stay up late and hear the close-of-play score in the Test Match at half past six?'

An equally famous case featured a young husband who had to rush his wife to hospital as she was expecting twins, possibly triplets. He wasn't allowed to stay with her and had to return home. After two or three hours he thought he'd better ring up the hospital to see if the twins, or possibly the triplets, had arrived. Without thinking he dialled the number of the Test Match answering service, something he did several times a day. Horrified, he heard a voice say, 'Three are out already, and the last two are ducks!'

Noel Ford has captured the husband-wife-cricket triangle perfectly. I only hope that some of the long-suffering cricket widows will think this book as funny as I do. I'm sure they will.

1. A group of clergymen (a breed not especially noted for its lack of interest in the game of cricket) now believes, in line with the Church's current soul-searching with regard to the accuracy of the Bible, that when God removed one of Adam's ribs in order to create Woman, Adam told Him that he'd prefer, God willing, so to speak, a cricket bat, and only changed his mind when God pointed out that, surely, he'd need someone to bowl to him, and anyway, who was going to make the sandwiches?

2. It is commonly believed that The Ashes are the burned remains of a bail, presented to the England captain following the defeat of Australia in the 1882/83 Test Match. This account is now in question following a scientific analysis which shows The Ashes to be the charred remains of two lamb chops and veg – presumably the remains of a meal cooked by one of the ladies for her husband, a member of the Australian team, which was ruined due to his late arrival home after the match.

3. If all the Cricket Widows in the world were laid end to end, their husbands wouldn't notice until the end of the cricket season.

4. Every two minutes a Cricketer's wife, somewhere, tells her husband to shut up about cricket. And the odds are, she's not the only one.

5. The other CND (The Cricket Neutralisation Directorate), is quietly gaining a foothold in some rural communities.

6. Anthropologists claim that Man's first significant breakthrough came when he discovered that he could use the bone of an animal as a tool. He would use it during the week to kill for food, then at the weekend use it to hit ball-shaped lumps of rock, during which activity the womenfolk would prepare the meat of the dead animals for consumption during the tea interval.

This view is supported by a new theory regarding the precise nature of Stonehenge.

7. The Samaritans receive 20,000 cricket-related calls a year. 10,000 are from wives, desperate to talk to someone, anyone, about something other than cricket. The other 10,000 are from husbands, desperate to know the latest Test score.

8. Psychiatrists specialising in cricket-related disorders use a special form of the 'ink blot' test to detect CWS (Cricket Widow Syndrome) in its early stages. Subjects are asked to study the 'ink blot', below, and to describe to the psychiatrist what they see.

A normal, well-adjusted woman will, of course, see a cricket ball. A potential CWS case, however, will see it as a bread-and-butter plate.

9. A cricketer who claimed that all wives really love cricket and that the number who didn't could stand on a pinhead, was crushed to death when they did.

FIRST INNINGS
The Cricketers Open

'Lucky devil! ... he's listening to the live Test
Match commentary from Australia'

'The lads were really complimentary about the
tea, Helen ... the least *I* could do was invite
them all back home for dinner'

'It should have been such a lovely wedding. The bride was all in white. Unfortunately, so was the groom, 150 miles away, playing cricket'

'I'm beginning to think that the only way I'll get
my husband to notice me is to rub in linseed oil
every day'

'The ball bounced, just inside the ropes, smashed
into Carol's teeth, up into the air and back down
onto her head. Damned bad luck … another eight
inches and it would have been a six'

20

'First he wants it this way, then he wants it that
way ... but ask him to help change the furniture
around at home ...'

21

'Why can't you hang your clothes up in the
wardrobe like any normal person?'

'How much longer are you going to be bowling
off your long run?'

'How could I possibly forget the day we met, dear? That wonderful, wonderful day in 1932, forever etched in my memory, when Verity took ten for ten in the Yorkshire v. Nottinghamshire match at Leeds'

'Make me a cup of tea, dear ... you can't imagine
what it's like to spend all day at the crease'

'The only reason your father helps with the washing up is because it helps him to practise his close fielding'

*'Try to talk your wife down ... she's the best
scorer the club's ever had'*

'Look, dear … his first googly!'

'You will meet a tall, dark stranger ... then you'll
remember ... it's your husband!'

'I knew it was a mistake, not cooking those
damned missionaries in the first place!'

'So, it's true, Gerald. You are completely
cricket mad!'

'He always gets out the same way … Legless-
Before-Wicket'

'Don't you think we should go home, dear?
There's really little hope, now, that the covers
will come off today'

'Ah! You must be the umpire … toss up, then,
and we'll decide who bats first'

'Is that it? Heaven is where bad light and rain
never stop play and a match never ends
in a draw?'

'What a wonderful view, dear ... from up here
you can see five different cricket matches!'

'We're quite happy to have the fathers present at
the birth, Mr Higgins, but I promise you, the
obstetrician doesn't need a close catcher'

Measuring up to Cricket Widowhood

This simple questionnaire, answered honestly, will confirm what Cricket Widows almost certainly already know.

Please Note: best results (from the point of view of accuracy, not necessarily peace of mind), will be obtained when the subject is completely relaxed and free from any stress. Under no circumstances, therefore, should the test be taken during the cricket season.

1. You are taking this test because:

(a) You bought this book yourself
(b) Your husband (or your best friend) bought it for you
(c) Your husband bought it for himself and you found it underneath his pillow.

2. After making love, your husband looks contentedly into your eyes and murmurs:

(a) 'How was it for you?'
(b) 'How was it for me?'
(c) 'HOWZTHAT!!!'

3. You are on holiday abroad when your husband's cricket club is scheduled to play a vital match. Your husband:

(a) Says, 'Ah well, they'll just have to manage without me for once'

(b) Says, 'I'm sorry, dearest, my club needs me. I must fly home for a couple of days'

(c) Doesn't say anything because he didn't come with you in the first place.

4. Your husband loves your eyes because:

(a) They're the same colour as his mother's

(b) They're the same colour as David Gower's

(c) They're usually the same colour as two cricket balls.

5. Your husband wants to buy a very expensive new cricket bat but you have seen a beautiful necklace which perfectly matches the earrings he gave you as a wedding present. Knowing that money is tight, he:

(a) Buys the necklace and tells you the bat can wait until next year

(b) Buys the bat and tells you the necklace can wait until next year

(c) Sells the earrings he gave you as a wedding present and uses the money to buy the bat.

6. You complain to your husband that he never takes you anywhere and tell him you're going home to mother. Without a moment's hesitation he:

(a) Takes you to the theatre

(b) Takes you to the Test Match

(c) Takes you to your mother and then goes to the Test Match.

7. Your husband comes home early from net-practice and catches you in bed with one of his club mates. By dint of a remarkable feat of will-power he controls his evident fury and splutters:

(a) 'How *could* you, dear!'

(b) 'How *could* you betray our friendship this way, Brian?'

(c) 'How *could* you skip net-practice, Brian – do you *know* how long I've been waiting for you down at the club?'

8. There is a cricket match on the television, and your young son, Darren, unwittingly moves between the screen and the chair from which your husband is viewing. Your husband leaps up and exclaims:

(a) 'Hey, Darren, you're blocking the screen!'

(b) 'Hey, watsaname, you're blocking the screen!'

(c) 'Hey, how long have we had a son?'

9. Your husband informs you that he has been invited to play in the club's six-week friendly tour of the West Indies. Your response on receiving this news is to:

(a) Agree that it's a once-in-a-lifetime opportunity and help him pack his things

(b) Reluctantly tell him you suppose he'd better pack his things and at least try to remember to send you a postcard

(c) Tear up the bloody postcard and telephone the police to cancel the Missing Person Search you requested five weeks ago.

10. It is the middle of the cricket season, a fine sunny Saturday afternoon and your husband, for reasons we need not discuss here, has gone for a stroll around the garden. As a direct result of this uncharacteristic behaviour:

(a) You decide that he can't be as fanatical about cricket as you imagined

(b) You telephone his doctor, suspecting a sudden and severe case of amnesia

(c) Your neighbours telephone the police to report a strange prowler next door.

11. You break the good news to your husband – you're pregnant! He:

(a) Rushes straight out to buy a dozen red roses for you
(b) Rushes straight out to buy a cricket bat for his new son
(c) Rushes straight out to buy a cricket bat for his new son and a bread-knife, cake recipe book and cricket score-pad just in case it turns out to be a girl.

12. Your husband carries your photograph with him wherever he goes because:

(a) You've written 'I Love You' on the front
(b) Viv Richards has signed his autograph on the back
(c) It reminds him who that odd but somehow familiar woman is who serves the teas down at the cricket club.

13. You are both in bed when your husband draws you to him, whispering endearments into your ear. You feign disinterest, suggesting that, these days, he seems to prefer cricket to you. In fact, you complain, as you continue to rebuff his advances, he is utterly obsessed with the game. Having digested this unexpected tirade, he:

(a) Pleads forgiveness for his thoughtlessness and swears that from now on, his only obsession will be you
(b) Denies he is obsessed but agrees he is quite keen on the game
(c) Goes into a sulk but finally agrees to take his cricket pads off.

14. Your husband tells you he's decided to give up cricket. You:

(a) Say 'Great!'
(b) Say 'Great – while it lasts!'
(c) Wake up.

15. You hear the sound of young boys playing outside. Suddenly a cricket ball smashes through your window and demolishes your best crystal vase. Your husband:

(a) Rushes out to give the boys a good telling off
(b) Murmers, 'Ah well, boys will be boys'
(c) Calls over the fence and asks you to throw the ball back.

16. The Marriage Guidance counsellor tells your husband, 'You have to make a very difficult decision: you can keep your cricket or you can keep your wife.' Your husband replies:

(a) 'I'll keep my wife'
(b) 'I'm sorry but I have to choose to keep my cricket'
(c) 'Yes, I realise that, but tell me more about this "very difficult decision".'

17. You have obviously suffered some kind of blackout. Consciousness slowly returns and, as you begin to take in your surroundings you realise that you are clutching a blood-stained cricket bat and your husband is lying motionless at your feet. You remember nothing, but your first thought is:

(a) My God! Intruders must have attacked my husband but I appear to have beaten them off with this cricket bat
(b) My God! My husband, finally realising that he has become hopelessly obsessed with cricket, has committed suicide. I must have snatched this bat from his hand whilst in a state of shock
(c) My God! I've done it again! Why do I keep marrying cricket freaks!

THE RATINGS

Score 0 points for every (a) answer.
Score 2 points for every (b) answer.
Score 5 points for every (c) answer.

(N.B. If you *refuse* to score on the grounds that you do enough of that every weekend at the cricket club then just award yourself 65 points.)

0-10 points: Go to your optician immediately. Either you misread the questions or you thought this book was about the effects of a decline in the male population of a species of grasshopper.

11-40 points: You are obviously a mere novice in the Cricket Widow stakes but stick around, you ain't seen nothin' yet!

41-65 points: Yes, you knew it all along, didn't you? You are a bona fide, 100%, gold medal Cricket Widow.

66-85 points: Don't worry ... yet! Keep very calm, and add up your score again. Right! Still the same? Are you sure that calculator is working properly? It is? All right, you can start to worry now, but *don't panic!* Perhaps you misread all of the questions? Unlikely? Hmmm ... this is going to take some time – why don't you go and have a nice quiet lie down for a few hours ... or a few days ... weeks ... months ...

SECOND INNINGS
The Cricket Widows Reply

'I just love the sound of leather against wood,
don't you?'

'It saves time, he's never out of them!'

'Now here it is once again, this time in slow
motion. Just look how that ball takes out
George's middle stump, making it the third time
in succession he's been out for a duck, first ball.
Here he goes, back to the pavilion, and I zoom
in onto his face. There it is, that familiar little
curl of the top lip as he scowls at the bowler ...'

'We'll never play this afternoon if this lot doesn't
let up soon, Samantha'

49

'Sorry chaps ... Alice has run off with the
laundry man'

'Who, me? ... er ... I'm the substitute!'

'Next time, dear, just send the twelfth man out
with the drinks'

'... and he's really running well between
the wickets ...'

'The way I heard it, after fifteen years of doing
the cricket teas, his wife finally snapped'

'I don't think I'll get changed to go home.
Jean's going through another one of her
aggressive phases'

'New wicket-keeping gloves? No, Janet locked
me out last night and slammed the window on
my hands when I tried to climb in'

*'I cleaned your cricket boots as you asked, dear
– they're on the chair'*

'Oh, well held, Caroline!'

'Give me a sporting chance, love ... pass me my
wicket-keeping gloves'

*'What … Oh, my God! … What did she put in
the sandwiches!'*

'I wondered why she kept giggling to herself all
the time she was knitting my new sweater'

'I just knew there had to be a better use for
tomatoes than making boring old sandwiches'

'Ah, I think someone must have been moving
behind the bowler's arm … yes, the umpire's
asking them to keep still until the over
is completed'

'We interrupt Test Match coverage with a News
Flash. A lady has just walked into her local
police station and admitted setting fire to her
house whilst her husband was inside watching
the cricket'

'We'd like to thank the lady who kindly sent our
commentators the gift of home-made toffee ...
Test Match coverage will resume as soon
as possible'

'Typical of a woman, hammering in with the
blade of the bat instead of the handle'

HELLO? — HELLO? — ARE YOU STILL THERE? YOU'LL HAVE TO SPEAK MORE CLEARLY — WHAT DID YOU SAY? — YOU'VE HAD YOUR BAILS WHIPPED OFF?...

Cricket Widows' Hand-Signals Explained

To the uninitiated, these esoteric gesticulations are a source of constant bafflement. Once explained, however, their meanings appear not only obvious but (unusually so for the female of the species) completely logical.

THE SIGNAL:
Index finger of one hand raised.

MEANING:
OUT. As in, 'You've got one minute to put down that stupid bat, phone the club to say that you can't make it this Sunday after all, get in the car and take me and the kids out!'

THE SIGNAL:
Both hands raised above head.

MEANING:
SIX. An indication to the cricketer of the estimated height, in feet, which the grass on the back lawn will reach by the end of the season if he intends playing cricket every bloody weekend.

THE SIGNAL:
Both arms extended outwards horizontally.

MEANING:
WIDE. This signal is open to two distinct interpretations. If the outstretched arms are accompanied by deep sighs and skyward cast eyes then the signaller is almost certainly a novice Cricket Widow, as yet unreconciled to her situa-

tion, and her gesture can be read as '"Whyd" you never stay home weekends?', '"Whyd" you never take me out any more?', etc.

On the other hand, this signal from an experienced and match-hardened Cricket Widow means, 'One more word about cricket and I'll stuff your bat down your throat – *this* way round!'

THE SIGNAL:
One arm extended outwards horizontally.

MEANING:
NO BALL. Here, the outstretched hand invariably points to Sunday's post-luncheon pile of dirty crockery and the threat is clear – 'No cricket match until that lot's done!', or 'No washing-up, no ball!'

THE SIGNAL:
Outstretched arm waved from side to side.

MEANING:
BOUNDARY. When a Cricket Widow is observed moving her arm in this manner, it is a sign that she has crossed that narrow boundary which divides normal and obsessive behaviour. Week after week of buttering slices of

bread for the teas has resulted in her buttering arm going into 'automatic spasm' and urgent medical help should be sought immediately the match is concluded and the players have had a chance to relax with a couple of pints.

THE SIGNAL:
Raising elbow and touching shoulder with hand.

MEANING:
ONE SHORT. The thirsty Cricket Widow's attempt to attract her husband's attention in the crowded club bar and to remind him that, when he's got in the team's third round of eleven pints of lager, she wouldn't mind a gin and tonic.

THE SIGNAL:
Raising leg and touching knee with hand.

MEANING:
This signal is rarely seen by the signee as, at this stage, he is usually bent double, legs crossed, with tears streaming through clenched eyelids. In view of this handicap, the action is normally

accompanied by the words, 'Just checking to see if you remembered to take your box off, dear – if it's any consolation, I hurt my knee too.'

THE SIGNAL:
Crossing the arms back and forth at knee level.

MEANING:
In the game of cricket, this signal means DEAD BALL. The Cricket Widow's version, however, means DEAD BORED. It first made its appearance in the 1920s when, in an attempt to relieve the boredom of their husbands' and boyfriends' cricket, thousands of flappers took up the Charleston.

THE SIGNAL:
Hand raised above head.

MEANING:
BYE. As in GOODBYE. As in, 'Goodbye-you-cretinous-cricket-crazy-creep-get-someone-else-to-spread-your-bread-wash-your-whites-and-polish-your-balls-because-when-you-get-home-I'll-be-away-and-if-our-paths-should-ever-cross-again-you'll-find-you're-on-a-very-sticky-wicket-because-I'll-shove-all-six-of-'em-complete-with-bails-where-you'll-need-an-umpire-with-obstetric-qualifications-to-draw-stumps!'

Last Day's Play

'Good heavens! ... that's the first time anyone's knocked the weather-vane off the pavilion roof since old Bradshawe in 1956'

'Would you believe that, in the excitement of
getting his MCC tie, he tied the knot too tightly?'

'How could she do it? The poor groundsman's
spent months getting this wicket right'

'Good grief, Betty … that's just the sort of pace
the Test Selectors are looking for'

'I think I'll ask for the heavy roller'

'What do you use to get the blood-stains out of
your husband's cricket whites?'

'The police said not to move the body so we might as well put him down as "retired hurt" and carry on with the game'

'Oh, Bill Smith's widow presented them to us after the cremation. She said he used to spend so much time here she didn't see why a small thing like death should break the habit of a lifetime'

'It's the first time I've ever prayed … I never
dreamt it would be answered so quickly!'

'Harry was a good sportsman, a keen cricketer
whose earthly innings were finally brought to a
close due to bad light ... he failed to see the
length of string tied across the top of the stairs'

Glossary of Terms in Common Use by Cricket Widows

RAIN STOPPED PLAY

Wet weather is often the cause of an unwelcome interruption in play. In particular, a heavy downpour can wash out a cricket match completely, resulting in the unexpectedly early return of a husband whose wife is 'in the covers'.

TAKING GUARD
A batsman should ensure that body and bat are positioned so that he can deal effectively with whatever form of attack the opposition may spring on him.

ATTACK
See above.

FLIGHT
What a wife should take following a successful attack which penetrates her husband's guard (see above).

PACE
See next item.

CAUGHT
What a wife gets if she hasn't enough pace.

BAIL

What any magistrate with a sense of justice, bearing in mind the extenuating circumstances, would grant the wife whose flight lacked pace and was caught.

APPEAL

What the wife must do if the magistrate doesn't have a sense of justice.

DUCK

A manoeuvre which, when successfully executed, will keep the cricketer out of a lot of trouble. More importantly, it will keep his wife out of a lot of trouble, too.

CHINAMAN

A specialist version of the bouncer – one who is skilled in Kung Fu and other forms of the martial arts.

LINE AND LENGTH

The line is what the cricketer's wife hangs the whites out on to dry, the length depends on whether she's been washing just the First XIs or the First XIs, Second XIs and Reserves.

IN THE COVERS
A popular position taken up, in close proximity to a male friend, by many wives whilst their husbands are otherwise occupied on the cricket pitch.

TIME WASTING
The term applied to many husbands to any activity that has no apparent connection with cricket.

L.B.W.
The League for Bored Wives.

ALL ROUNDER

An expression used to describe the figure of husbands who insist on their wives waiting on them hand and foot whilst they stay glued to the television coverage of the Test series.

HAT TRICK

An amusing practical joke played by Cricket Widows with their husband's safety helmet and a tube of super-glue.

BOUNCER

Another method devised by Cricket Widows of a more sensitive disposition for keeping their husbands at home.

THE FIFTY PARTNERSHIP

Otherwise known as the Golden Wedding Anniversary, this target is seldom achieved by Cricket Widows.

DOLLY CATCH
Something which many cricketers hope to make after the match, usually by the ploy of cornering their prey and reducing them to a state of catatonic immobility with endless boring accounts of their prowess on the field.

GROPING
One of the objectives of the player attempting to make a dolly catch. (Definitely not to be confused with the well known cricketing phrase, 'A safe pair of hands'.)

N.B. The unexpected appearance of a wife (or the young lady's husband), invariably leads to the player fumbling the attempt.

SWEEP
See next item.

FOLLOW ON
When they have finished washing-up, putting things away, stacking the chairs, sweeping the floor etc etc, the wives are permitted to follow on to the club bar, where their husbands have been since the match ended. Given more than their average share of luck, they will find (a) The bar is still open and (b) Their husbands, having failed to make a dolly catch, are still there.

LEG BREAK
A simple but extremely effective method adopted by some wives in an attempt to keep their husbands at home during the cricket season.

SHORT LEG
A medical condition found in husbands whose wives have used the 'leg-break' ploy once too often.

STUMPED

A medical condition found in husbands whose wives have used the 'leg-break' ploy *more* than once too often.

LONG HOP

The journey between home and the cricket club for a husband suffering from either of the above two medical conditions.

WALKING

What the cricketer has to do when his wife has accidentally fed his car keys to the dog.

STONE-WALLING
The last resort of Cricket Widows for whom all the previous methods have failed.

TAIL-ENDER
A particularly fine stroke from an experienced Cricket Widow. Also known as 'Caught behind'.

MAIDEN OVER